Finding Love

Jessica Lara

2
Finding Love

Jessica Lara

Foreword

"If you're asking if I need you, the answer is forever, if you are asking if I'll leave you, the answer is never, if you are asking what I value, the answer is you, if you are asking if I love you, the answer is I do."

"- Unknown"

4

Finding Love

Jessica Lara

Chapter One

"You can't be serious" Elizabeth said in dismay.

"We need food; an as of now it looks like we have probably less than two days worth of food before we run out. I can't live like this anymore Lizy, and you can't either," Joshua replied.

"But what if you…"

"Don't worry, I won't get caught and if I do… let's face it, you'll have one less extra weight lifted off your shoulders."

"What are you talking about, you're the only thing I have left to live for. You're like the brother

Finding Love

I've always wanted and needed in my life," Elizabeth yelled.

The very thought of Joshua being caught, made her dizzy and Elizabeth began to cry.

"Please Lizy, don't cry," Joshua said as he stretched out his arms to embrace her, Elizabeth went willingly. Joshua was the only family she had left, he was her world.

"I don't know what I'd do without you," Elizabeth said sadly.

The rain began to softly hit the roof.

"Lizy, I'm really sorry," he whispered in her ear slipping from her grasp, he ran out the door and into the night. Elizabeth started to pace, worrying about what reckless things he would do. She sat down on the cot. The very thought of something bad happening to her adopted brother caused her heart to race and suddenly she was very dizzy. Lying down on the cot, she hugged the pillow as tears continued to roll down her cheeks. Her mind began to wonder to the past, to the beginning.

***

Jessica Lara

"GIVE IT BACK!" Elizabeth cried, as she run after the boy who took her doll.

"You have to catch me if you can, crybaby," said the boy,

"I am not a crybaby," Elizabeth yelled back at him as she continued to chase him along the bank of the river, but suddenly she tripped falling on her face. Finding her footing, she realized it was a young boy she had tripped over. He was very grimy, with dirty-blonde hair and deep blue eyes. His slender build revealed strong features and a very kind face.

"Are you all right?" he asked in a deep, calm voice.

Elizabeth immediately snapped back to reality and stuttered, "y-yes."

"What's your name," he asked.

"Elizabeth but may family calls me Lizy; and you? What's your name?"

"I... I... I... I'm..." He stuttered.

"Oh, come on out with it" Elizabeth retorted.

"My name is Joshua!" he snapped.

8

Finding Love

***

As the sun began to appear over the horizon, Elizabeth rose, washed her face and started her normal routines. First things first she thought. Getting water from the well and feeding the chickens, gathering eggs, and harvesting the vegetables for sale at the market which wasn't her idea of fun but it was a needful thing. She glanced up towards the palace and saw a crowd but didn't think much about it. Elizabeth realized that if she and Joshua were to survive they had to stick together and do what must be done. She continued feeding the chickens when it suddenly hit her, Joshua! What if they caught Joshua? She dropped the seeds grabbed the end of her skirt and ran with all her might. Running up the hill, through the town, across the bridge, and over to the palace. When she reached the palace she saw the crowd of people and a small band of guards and between all them was Joshua.

"No" Elizabeth yelled. Still running she pushed

Jessica Lara

herself through the crowd toward Joshua. Elizabeth threw herself between Joshua and the guards. She fastened her eyes on their prisoner and no one else.

"Please, tell me what have he done that he would deserve this" she said with renewed tears in her eyes.

Holding on to the guard's arm Elizabeth began pleading for Joshua's life. "Please, we are not in the days of old, you can't do this, and he is entitled to a trial". Elizabeth looked to the crowd for support in her plea but no one stepped forward. "Can't you see this is wrong", she yelled at the crowd, "together we can make them stop this barbaric practice! They can just take us off the street and execute us at their whim; we are entitled to a fair trial. Again facing the guards, please: take me instead; he is the only family I have left". Regardless of her plea, the guard continued to push Joshua not allowing him to rise from the ground. The second guards stepped aside allowing the executioner to pick the weapon that would kill Joshua.

Finding Love

It was at that moment, Elizabeth noticed the Prince standing in the background. She threw herself at his feet. "Your majesty, please do not let them take my brother's life. I offer myself for his crimes." This remark caused the executioner to halt his assault on Joshua as he looked to the prince for instructions. His axe was held up high over the very neck of his prisoner; Joshua's eyes were closed as if he were ready to die.

Jessica Lara

Chapter Two

Joshua recognizing Elizabeth's voice opened his eyes and looked up at her. His expression was happy but then it suddenly turned sad. Elizabeth crawled over to Joshua's side, kissing his face she tried to reassure him everything will be alright.

"They could kill you for this," he said "please don't do this. I can't let you die for me."

"Don't worry I've got this in the bag!" Elizabeth stated.

"How do you propose to save the both of us?" he asked

Finding Love

"Well, I don't know yet but I'll think of something!" Elizabeth whispered as she stood up to face Prince Mark. Although his facial expression never wavered, the prince could not take his eyes off the vision that was standing before him. She stood very erect never blinking and challenging. Never had he witness this type of strength in a woman. She challenged him, yet gave him the respect due his title. It was then that Elizabeth took her first clear look at the prince. He had this look that made everything around her go away. Taking in the very sight of him, she noticed his black somewhat curly hair, which complemented his pale skin and blue eyes. He was a slight bite older then her but not too much. Elizabeth couldn't help but think of how gorgeous he was! Elizabeth had heard a lot about Prince Mark before, but never had the chance to see him herself until now.

"Guard; lower your weapon…" Prince Mark ordered the guard, never losing his focus of her. Hearing the prince's orders, the executioner slowly lowered the axe. Prince Mark walked towards her. Elizabeth just stood there unaware what to do.

Jessica Lara

Looking quickly down at Joshua, "would you die for this thief?" Prince Mark demanded.

Elizabeth looked first at Joshua noticing that his eyes were once again closed and she realized that he was uttering a prayer. Looking back to the prince, "yes I would." she paused and repeated with conviction "Yes I would!"

Immediately Joshua stopped praying and slowly looked up at her. Not blinking, Elizabeth continued to stare in the eyes of the prince. It was there she could see the look of confusion combined with the sense of being lost and a little surprise. Within her mind she wondered why all these expressions would come across his face. He was the prince and in the absence of the king, he was in charge. Elizabeth figured he had seen everything imaginable within his kingdom. But she guessed he couldn't believe anyone would actually say that. Prince Mark looked back and forth between Elizabeth and Joshua, as if he was attempting to figure out something.

"I'll make you a deal...free the boy" Prince Mark said.

Finding Love

Immediately, the guards stood Joshua up and removed the chains that bound him. Rubbing his wrists where the chains were, he straggled to Elizabeth's side facing the prince. "What's the catch?" Elizabeth asked defiantly.

The guards paused… and looked up at Elizabeth.

"You have to be my servant and live with me in the palace for the space of two years!"

"No she can't do that, I won't let her", yelled Joshua.

"I guess you are willing to die for your crimes then. Take him" the prince demanded of the guards.

As the guard again grabbed Joshua, the executioner pulled up the axe yet again.

"No! Wait! I will do it" Elizabeth yelled while reaching out to stop the executioner arms. The guard stopped and looked again at the prince for directions.

"Okay then, it's settled, you are to move in immediately, and he has to find a job." Prince Mark turning towards Joshua, "if I ever find out that you have returned to the life of crime there

Jessica Lara

will be no second chance. Remember, your sister will make restitution for you in this case." With this declaration, he turned and mounted his horse, looking down from his perch "I never caught your name. What did you say it was?"

"I didn't. It's Elizabeth; Elizabeth Clarisse Bailly" she said defiantly.

"Alright Ms. Elizabeth Clarisse Bailly, my footman will bring you to the palace and escort you to your quarters!" Looking to the right, Elizabeth saw the guy he was talking about. Erick, the footman probably in his early 20s was standing holding the door to the coach that always follows the prince. He was tanned, muscularly built, with jet dark black hair and green eyes. Erick didn't smile nor offer any additional communication as Elizabeth stepped towards the coach. Joshua pulled at her arms, pleading with her not to go. "I must, we made a deal with the prince. It won't be long. I can do two years standing on my head". Remember, you have to get a job and maybe, just maybe you will be able to come visit me. I am sure I will have days off that we can get together maybe takes in a show or just

Finding Love

get a cup of coffee. Besides I have never heard the prince being too unfair to his employees. Now we know he hates thieves. I love you Jo-Jo, be good and please stay out of trouble." Elizabeth boarded the coach as Erick closed the door and stood on the back foot railing. The groomsman shook the reins and the horses started off towards the castle.

***

Jessica Lara

Chapter Three

Arriving at the palace, "follow me..." Erick said as he jumped down from the back of the coach and walked toward the palace. He then directed Elizabeth into the foyer and up the stairs. It appeared they walked three or four miles as they traveled down many halls before finally reaching a bedroom at the end of the hall.

"If there's anything you need..." Erick began as he opened the door and allowed Elizabeth to walk in. "Just ask!" He finished.

"Thank you, I think I am alright right now..."

Finding Love

Elizabeth began as she walked into the room. She stopped short, the room was so beautiful! More beautiful then anything she had ever seen. In her mind she wondered if all the servants had rooms such as this.

"Miss Elizabeth?" Erick asked getting her attention.

"Please forgive me, there is something I have to ask, where and when will I get my uniforms and do all the servants live like this?"

"Ha, ha, ha servant? You're hilarious!" Erick laughed loudly.

"What's so funny?" Elizabeth asked very annoyed.

"Prince Mark can be a tyrant at times and even a little cruel if he wants. But he's not going to make you be his servant. He says that to scare you. He's really never come across anyone that would actually put their life on the line for someone else like you did today. No need for you to worry he wouldn't make you be his servant. You're his guest and you'll be treated like one. Welcome. Remember if you need anything just ask!" Erick

Jessica Lara

replied. "Oh yeah, the servants have different quarters, not as grand as this but it will do okay in a pinch."

"Thank you Erick. I will remember!" Elizabeth said "but I am so very confused. Why would the prince want me to be a guest? Sure you said no one ever put their life of the line, but why me?"

"Ms Elizabeth, I can see you have not taken a good look at yourself lately" was the reply Erick gave as he walked out and closed the door behind him.

The evening stretched on forever. Elizabeth really didn't know what to do with herself. So she explored the room. In the center of the room stood a very large four post bed, larger than any bed she had ever seen. To the right of the bed was a large closet that ran from ceiling to floor. Walking across the room, Elizabeth found the bathroom. It was larger than her small cottage. There she found a garden tub with all types of bath oils and soaps, miles of towels of every size and color. Behind the door was a white plush bathrobe. The vanity had all types of lotions, perfumes, face creams and

Finding Love

makeup. It was getting late, Elizabeth suddenly felt tired. The events of the day had finally taken its toll. Spontaneously, she decided to take a bath. What could be the harm she thought? Just as quickly, she striped while the water was running in the tub, without thinking she selected the lavender bubble bath and poured a liberal amount into the tub. Without hesitation she stepped into the scented bath and lost herself among the bubbles. Time stood still, Elizabeth was lost in her own thoughts. The scent of the water and the events of the day caused her to become sleepy. Getting out of the tub, she toweled herself dry and put on the robe and walked back into the room. On a rolling cart besides the bed was a tray full of food. Elizabeth had never seen so much in one setting. There was a bottle of wine, Cornish hen, wild rice, sauté vegetables, rolls and butter. For desert the tray displayed strawberry cheese cake and coffee. The one thing that caught her eyes was a glass with one long stem red rose. Sitting on the bed, smelling the food, she realized how hungry she was. She couldn't resist and began eating with relish. Finishing her meal, the door suddenly opened and in walked a young girl just a few years younger than herself. "Good evening miss, I am so glad you enjoyed your meal" she said lightly. The prince asked that you come to see him as soon as feel up to it. He will be in the Library."

Elizabeth quickly redressed, "so where is the library?" she asked.

"Go down the hall turn right and take the stairs, the library should be on your left when you get at the end of the stairs. Have a good evening miss." Following the young girls' instructions Elizabeth arrived at the library in record time. She knocked on the door and waited.

***

Instead of the prince telling her to come, he opened the door and allowed Elizabeth to follow him into the room. As he walked, he said "I trust you found your quarters acceptable".

"Yes, thank you" she replied.

"Please, sit Ms Elizabeth Clarisse Bailly; I will be

Finding Love

with you in a moment."

Sitting behind his desk, the prince returned to business at hand. He was reading over the business affairs of the township, and reviewing the budget. Elizabeth sat fidgeting in her chair. She was anxious to see what the prince wanted from her. How long will he keep me waiting she thought? I am not sure what he expects of me but he will be sadly mistaken if he thinks I am going to be his little play toy. I wonder why he told me I will be his servant yet Erick said I was his guest, I hope he will hurry up and tell me what the conditions of me being here are. All these thoughts ran quickly through her mind. She shifted again and let out a loud sigh. The prince looked up from his papers and said "are you bored, Ms Elizabeth Clarisse Bailly?"

"Your majesty, I wish you would stop calling me by my entire name, since I am here now please I prefer that you call me Lizy and yes I am getting a little bored. I am also curious as to why I am here and what is expected of me. You told me that I was to be your servant, yet your footman said I was

Jessica Lara

your guest. You must understand that I do have a home, chickens and a vegetable garden I must take care of. For two years, how do you expect that my house and belongs will survive, thieves will come in and take everything my brother and I have. I must make sure that my brother is alright and..."

" Ms Elizabeth Clarisse Bailly, sorry I mean Lizy, please take a breath, I promise everything thing will be revealed to you soon, your property will be taken care of and your brother is at home so no thief will come in. As for this what is required of you, I believe that I said you will be my servant for two years".

"Yes you did say that, but servants have their own quarters and I promise I will not be your play toy to discard after two years. I..."

"**Ms Elizabeth Clarisse Bailly**, I want you to know that my intentions are strictly honorable. Please do not try my patients with worthless verbal debates. I will not have you challenge me. What I require of you for the next two years is to be my escort in society. I am negotiating pact with several different countries and I need someone of

Finding Love

your standards to accompany me as I travel around the country side and sometime aboard. After the two year period your virtues will still be intact and you can go back to your little cottage in the woods. Now if you excuse me I have urgent business to attend". The prince rose from his chair, dismissing Elizabeth who ran from the room even more confused from her encounter with the prince.

Jessica Lara

Chapter Four

The next day she arose to a sudden clatter.

"All right miss, its time to get up and get going… oh, sorry; how rude of me. I'm Petra and while you are here I will be the one that will assist you in getting ready for every event."

"Hi…. I'm Elizabeth" Elizabeth said as she slowly opened her eyes to see a young girl probably no older then her. She had light brown curly hair pulled back into a tight side ponytail and light brown eyes. She wore a black solid dress that made her light skin look even prettier. You are not the same person that came in yesterday. Did I do something to cause her not to come back" Elizabeth asked sleepily.

"No madam, that was Gail, she was just helping out. I have been busy shopping for your outfits and jewelry and also I had to ensure that the makeup would complement your beautiful skin. It's been a long time since I had so much fun shopping. I just hope that I got all the right sizes, the prince gave me your size he has a very good eye. I have never known him to be wrong about anything. So let's get moving young lady since you are Prince Mark's guest! I have your dress for today's activities, and the rest of your clothes should be here later this afternoon in time for you to get ready".

"Please tell... What am I getting ready for" Elizabeth asked confused.

"Your introduction to the ruling class and eventually you will be escorting the prince to dinner at Earl White gate's villa this evening. Anything else I can answer?'

"Oh nothing more, I was just wondering."

"Come on Elizabeth, let's get up! We have so

Jessica Lara

much to do. First you have to take a shower. Then there's your hair and make-up and we still have to make sure I chose the right dress with jewelry and shoes to match. We cannot afford to waste a second." Elizabeth groaned inwardly and thought just go with the flow two years won't be too long. She forced herself out of bed and stumble her way into the shower. Although she preferred the bath, she didn't want to keep Petra waiting. Almost immediately she was rushed right away into a chair and the magic began. Petra brushed her thick auburn hair into a high French roll, and allowing some of the tresses' to fall curling each with the hot iron and letting them fan her face she sprayed lots of hair spray. She then applied a light foundation, some eye shadow, blush, eyeliner, lip-gloss, mascara. Working quickly and efficiently Petra takes a few steps back to look at Elizabeth fully. Her eyes have a little shimmer in them and she is smiling as if she's unbelievably happy with herself.

"Princess, you look...I mean...Miss Elizabeth, you look amazing."

Finding Love

Elizabeth thought to herself, yeah right, there is no possible way I can look that good, getting up she walk over to the mirror. There is not enough makeup that could change this plain old; -- holy smokes Elizabeth couldn't believe the vision of loveliness in the mirror. She looked at herself spinning around side to side. Suddenly she felt just like a princess.

"Whoa..." Elizabeth said in a whisper.

Her eyes, they stood out, they've never had looked so green. And her hair! Petra curled it slightly and given her side bangs that made it just look like...WOW. She turned and looked at Petra with her eyes wide.

"Well...?" Petra asks.

Unable to contain herself, Elizabeth ran threw her arms around Petra laughing and in the same breath said "I love it. Thank you."

Joining in on the laughter and hugs Petra said "You're very welcome. I knew you would love it and now for your dress."

From the closet Petra brings out the loveliest green dress Elizabeth had ever seen. As she places it on the bed Elizabeth immediately runs over to it. Almost too afraid to touch the dress she whispers "oh my, it's so beautiful!" As an afterthought, she then touches her cheeks just beneath her left eye. "It's the same color as my eyes!"

Knowingly Petra smiles and said "now quickly! We don't have much time, put it on!"

Elizabeth nods and quickly drops the bathrobe and steps into the dress, turning so that Petra could secure the zipper. The dress fit like a glove, she notice the cut was perfect to allow just a slight hint of cleavage being shown and it was tapered at the waist to allow for her perfect shape to be displayed. Petra had laid out the perfect matching earrings and necklace and next to the bed was matching shoes. She put everything on and went to stand once again in front of the mirror. Viewing herself she instantly thought I wonder what the Prince will think of me. "Oh my, why am I thinking such thoughts, it really doesn't matter, and I will only be here for two years" she chastened herself. Shaking her head "It shouldn't matter because I don't care." she thought again. "Well it wouldn't hurt if he did like it. Would it?"

She then took one more glance at herself once more before heading downstairs. With all the courage she could muster up she lifted her head high and said "Okay Elizabeth on with the show".

***

When she reached bottom of the stairs Prince Mark had his back to the stairs talking with Prince Henry of Norway. Glancing over the room, Elizabeth noticed everyone around appeared to be royalty; dukes, duchesses, lords, and ladies. Each were talking holding glasses and having a wonderful time. Elizabeth felt completely lost, but pride made her continue into the room. She noticed that others begun noticing her. Not wanting to appear to be unaware of what was required of her she continued into the room. She had attempted to catch Prince Mark's attention while not losing the air of sophistication, but then realize that she was probably looking even more out of place. Her next thought was to stand still and see if others would come to her. She started to feel as if she had stood rooted for hours. She turned to walk away she felt a hand grab her wrist finding her captor to be Prince Mark.

"Now where do you think you're going?" Prince Mark said as he pulled her toward the big crowd. "Ladies and gentleman may I have your attention, I would like you to meet Elizabeth." He said as he put his arm around her waist.

Elizabeth didn't know what to say or do, she was lost, confused, nervous and freezing cold. She looked at the crowd for awhile. They were just staring at her. "Did I do something wrong? Is there something on my face? What is it?" Questions spun through her head as she tried to figure out what to do.

"Good day to you" Elizabeth said as she curtsied grabbing the Prince's hand.

Prince Mark looked over at her and smiled a weird yet so adorable crooked smile.

Each member of the royal court returned the greeting with a curtsy or a bow and immediately returned to their conversation with each other

Finding Love

again. All of a sudden, she felt neglected. She wanted to scream at the top of her lungs but that would have been out of place in the royal setting, she needed fresh air. "I am going to go get some air, I'll be right back."

"Okay, I will accompany you…"

"No… really you need to stay with the guest. I'll be back I promise."

Releasing the prince's hand, Elizabeth walked out the French doors and into the garden. The garden was amazing, every flower was in bloom. The fragrance was overwhelming but very comforting. She wondered around the garden until she came to the east side of the palace and saw a maze. The desire to explore the maze was more than she could resist. Glancing back at the palace, she thought I should have enough time for a walk through. Without hesitation she stepped into the maze. At first the maze was fun, every twist lead to something exciting, but then she became frightened; noises were coming from every direction. Turning around in circles everything looked alike. Frightened; Elizabeth began to run

Jessica Lara

back towards where she believed she started in the maze. All of a sudden, the noises became louder and closer causing her to frantically search for the exit. She didn't know what was happening, she didn't know where she was going, and was too scared to stop. She then glanced back for a short second before running into something that was very solid and with strong arms that immediately wrapping around her. Letting out a small squeal, she fought with all her might. With his lips meeting hers, she then realized it was just the Prince and returned his kiss. She felt safe now but at the same time more frighten than she was when she was alone in the maze. Placing his arm under her knees, he lifted her up to his chest and began the walk out of the maze. Exiting the maze, Erick stood at the door with a concerned look. He whispered something in the prince's ear. Ringing the servant bell brought Petra to the hall, "please take Elizabeth to her room, I have an emergency I must attend to" said the prince as he and Erick departed through a side door.

Finding Love

Chapter Five

Her lips were still tingling from the kiss Elizabeth sat down on the bed. With a questioning look at Petra who was just looking down at her feet.

"Petra?" Elizabeth asked in a short questioning tone.

"Yes?" Petra asked looking at her.

"I know this maybe none of my business. But I'm curious. Would you know what the emergency was?"

"Well it was nothing of national importance I believe its probably just something about King

Jessica Lara

George's heath."

"Will you tell me?"

"You probably think it's boring and you need to get some rest."

"Oh please tell me, please. Come on I'm going to either get the news the hard way or the easy way. Either you're going to tell me, or since I'm going to be staying here for awhile, I think I'll figure it out by the rumors." Elizabeth said with a smirk across her face.

"Oh, all right. Well not long ago King George became very ill. Everyone believed he would eventually get better but we were wrong. We don't know what's going to happen next. But whatever it is. It probably will not be anything good. And now King William and Queen Myra are on their way right now over to the palace to see him and Prince Mark."

"I thought it was Queen Mary?"

"No not anymore. See when Prince Mark and Prince George were young adults, Queen Mary died of pneumonia. It wasn't long before King William found a new love and moved on. King

Finding Love

William then decided to move his new wife Queen Myra and himself to the country and leave Prince George and Prince Mark here alone. Prince George then became King George and Mark he stayed Prince Mark. King William spent many years with Queen Myra until now, since he has got notice that King George hasn't been doing well and he will pass the crown over to Prince Mark."

"Oh, I guess that explains it all." Elizabeth said.

"Okay now I have told you all I know; now you need to get some rest." Petra said as she stood up and walked towards the door.

"Tell me more." Elizabeth said curiously.

"Goodnight Elizabeth!" Petra said switching the lights off. Sitting on the bed, Elizabeth knew she couldn't sleep, there was too much activity going on downstairs and she was concerned about Prince Mark. Slipping out of bed, she creped down the stairs.

***

"Mark, my baby" Queen Myra shrieked as she

Jessica Lara

entered the palace.

Prince Mark looked at the door looking for his father.

"Where's father?" Mark asked still looking at the palace doors.

"Mark darling, I am so sorry. As we were coming here bandits pulled the carriage over and killed him. The driver and I were lucky enough to get away and hide. When they left we got back into the carriage and drove over here as fast as we could. I am so sorry Mark. The guards are taking his body to the family crypt."

Prince Mark just looked at Myra stunned, confused, sad, and lost. It was impossible for him to say anything.

His father was gone and his brother was very ill and he was soon to be king. Elizabeth felt so bad.

"Mark, who's that?" Queen said looking beyond Mark and at Elizabeth standing on the stairs.

Turning to look over his shoulders, Mark said, "Myra, this is Elizabeth, Elizabeth this is Queen Myra, my stepmother."

Without reservation, Elizabeth extended her

Finding Love

hand to the Queen and then thought better of it, with a quick curtsy she said "your highness, it's a pleasure to meet you. I am so sorry about what happened to you and King William. Please let me know if I can do anything for you".

Queen Myra looked up and down at Elizabeth before turning to Prince Mark.

"I'm starved, what are we having for dinner? Have Emily bring something to my quarters, I am going to lie down." Queen Myra said with a commanding nod.

***

The rest of the evening passed without an incident, Prince Mark went into the library and Erick followed him. Elizabeth returned to her room unsure what she needed to do next. She suddenly was aware of how hungry she was. Being lost in the maze had caused her to miss dinner and with the appearance of the Queen and the news of King William the palace was in an uproar. Everyone was running around as Prince Mark ordered the guard to find the bandits that had anything to do with the death of his father. The sound of her stomach caused Elizabeth to once again travel down the stairs searching for the kitchen. Following the smells Elizabeth found the kitchen and walked in on the servants talking about Queen Myra. "She is the biggest gold digger I have ever seen" said one of the maids polishing the silver. "I don't understand what King William saw in the woman, she is evil through and through" said Emily the cook. "Imagine ordering me to bring her food to her quarters, she has a maid-in-waiting to do that for her" she kept talking. "That poor child, I know she hates working with that witch" the maid replied. Laughter erupted for the rest of the staff. "Excuse me" Elizabeth said shyly.

Emily wiping her hands on her apron, "sweet Jesus, baby what are you doing here?" "I got a little hungry and I thought if it's not too much trouble, I could get something eat" Elizabeth replied.

"Why didn't you ring the bell in your quarters, Petra would have brought you a tray to your room" the maid replied. "I really don't want to be any

Finding Love

trouble, Petra has enough to do, believe me, it's much easier for me to come here, if you don't mind" replied Elizabeth. "Baby it's no problem, come sit here and I'll get you something post-haste" said Emily. "I take it, Queen Myra isn't your favorite person, I'm sorry I shouldn't be leading you in to kitchen gossip, but I couldn't help but overhear what you were saying" said Elizabeth. "Please don't take offense", said the maid, you are a quest here and we are servants and we should be careful what we say, please forgive us for gossiping about the Queen". "Please consider me as being one of you guys, Prince Mark told me that I was to be his servant for two years. I know that from the look I received from Queen Myra this evening, we are not going to be best friends, no matter how long I am to be here at the palace." Elizabeth told the staff. Ironically, the talk in the kitchen took on a different venue while Elizabeth finished eating.

Chapter Six

"Miss Elizabeth?" Petra said.

"Yes!"

"Prince Mark wanted to know if you're ready!" Petra said.

"Yes, yes I am" Elizabeth stated.

Petra walked in the room and stood behind Elizabeth as she just sat staring at herself in the mirror.

"You look beautiful" Petra said.

"Thank you." Elizabeth said smiling at Petra.

"You remind me of Holly. She used to sit in the

Finding Love

front of the mirror every morning, just to make sure she looked perfect!"

"Holly, tell me who is Holly?" Elizabeth asked as she turned around to look at Petra.

"Holly was the Prince's first love; beautiful, smart, everything required to be the next queen. She and Prince Mark dated last summer for awhile. He had just started to fall for her too, until she was found sleeping with married man."

"My goodness, what happened to Holly?"

"She was sentenced to death."

"Oh my, so how did the Prince take the news and everything that happened?"

"He was devastated by it. He couldn't believe it. He had given pretty much his whole life to her and she threw it all away. That's why it is said he probably won't fall in love again."

"Oh, so he won't get married ever?" Elizabeth asked curiously turning slowly to face the mirror again.

"Marriage is something he has to do in order to sit on the throne. I think Queen Myra will find the right girl to be queen." Petra stated.

Jessica Lara

"Oh my." Elizabeth said as she looked up into the mirror doubtfully.

Petra just looked at Elizabeth's expression but did not question her concerning.

"Well we better get you down stairs, the Prince is waiting."

"Yes of course, we must not keep the Prince waiting."

Elizabeth went downstairs to the dinner room to find Prince Mark and Queen Myra waiting.

"Good evening Lizy" Prince Mark said.

"Your majesty, Queen Myra how are you this evening?" Elizabeth curtsied.

"Sit please!"

"Thank you!"

Elizabeth sat down at one end of the table while Prince Mark sat at the other end with Myra at his left.

"So are you settling down and tell me how do you like it here?" Prince Mark asked Elizabeth.

"Well sire, it is..." She began.

"It's great being back in the palace again, oh how I missed this place. How's it been up here without

Finding Love

me?" Myra ruddily interrupted her.

"Dinner is served," Erick said coming out of the kitchen followed by a few butlers with trays laden with food. Elizabeth eyes opened wide, there was enough to feed a small army and yet there were only three people at the table.

With much flair, Erick placed her napkin in her lap, leading close to Elizabeth. "Thank you" Elizabeth said.

"You're quite welcome and if you need anything else please don't hesitate to ask!" He whispered in her ear.

"I'll keep that in mind." she said with a smile.

"Please enjoy your meal" Erick said standing up straight and walking back into the kitchen.

During the course of the meal, Prince Mark spoke quietly almost to himself. "Well I have some news," Prince Mark said looking down at his plate picking at his food.

"I am sorry dear I could barely hear you, what kind of news?" Myra asked.

"Bad" Prince Mark replied.

"Please don't keep me in suspense, what's the

news then?" Myra said with a lighter tone this time.

"It's concerning the King." He said looking down the table. Elizabeth just nodded. And then he began telling the rest of the story.

"And well, we thought George would get better. But it seems whatever this is, is taking its toll" Prince Mark began while putting his fork and knife down and looking up. "We don't think he's going to make it."

"Oh my, I'm so..." Elizabeth began.

"Why didn't you tell me this earlier, I must go and see him at once." Queen Myra exclaimed as she interrupted Elizabeth once more.

"I'd thought it better to tell you both at the same time."

Queen looked at Prince Mark as he picked his fork and knife and began to eat again and then looked down at Elizabeth. Elizabeth immediately picked up her fork and began to eat. When she looked at Queen Myra she noticed such an evil look but did not understand the reasoning behind the stare.

Finding Love

"It's important to me that both of you be here to know what I have planned. If anything happens, I need Elizabeth to accommodate me through the process. It will be important that our subject be aware that King's family is still in touch with them and that everything that George started I intend to continue. My father and my brother will be remembered as kings of the people."

Elizabeth just sat there and looked at Prince Mark. She noticed the door to the kitchen was ajar and all of the servants were eaves dropping on the conversation. Elizabeth smiled then looked back at Prince Mark.

"Are you asking me to pose as your wife?" Elizabeth said trying to make Myra jealous.

"Yes, but only if you wish it to be like that!" replied Prince Mark

"Sure, I don't mind" said Elizabeth stealing a look at Myra.

Queen Myra looked at Elizabeth and Elizabeth returned her stare, and even flashed a big fake smile. Without a second thought she returned to eating.

Jessica Lara

"Good it's settled. Well it's good that you're going with me and not..."

"I know what you mean." Elizabeth stated not letting him finish.

Elizabeth looked at the kitchen door witnessing Erick and Petra jumping up and down. Elizabeth smiled eating her food with a greater appreciation. As soon as the meal was finished, the prince, queen and Elizabeth moved to the drawing room. Prince allowed Queen Myra walk ahead.

"Excuse me. Elizabeth?"

"Yes!" Elizabeth turned facing Prince Mark.

"Come with me let's take a walk in the garden?"

It wasn't exactly what she was hoping he was going to say but it was close enough.

Prince Mark and Elizabeth were walking through the garden. The walk did not include talking but enjoying the night air and the silence of their own company. Soon what appeared to be a dead end led to a little park and a white gazebo. Stopping and looked over at each other.

"Would you care to dance?" Prince Mark asked.

There was nothing but silence till Elizabeth found

Finding Love

a response.

"But there's no music for dancing." She said.

"What? Are you afraid?" he said trying to intimidate her.

"No!" She stated.

"Do you not know how to dance?"

"Of course I know how to dance."

"Then where's no problem.

"There's no music!"

"Come, let's make our own music" Prince grabbed Elizabeth's hand walking onto the gazebo.

Prince Mark then grabbed her waist and began to dance a very slow waltz. After a while Elizabeth looked up at Prince Mark, as Prince Mark looked down at her. Slowly they stopped dancing and looked deeply into each other's eyes. Prince Mark leaned in cupping Elizabeth's face. They were interrupted by a voice.

"Prince Mark! Prince Mark!" Erick yelled a he ran down the pathway.

Prince Mark then looked over at Erick.

"Prince Mark. I am so sorry to interrupt you but its King George. He said he needed to talk with you

Jessica Lara

immediately."

Prince Mark looked back at Elizabeth.

"Go, he needs you!" Elizabeth said.

"Thank you." Prince Mark replied walking off the gazebo. He slowly let go of her hands and then ran down the pathway back to the Palace. Elizabeth stood there watching Prince Mark running until she could no longer see him.

Without his presence, the night was even darker, so she decided to go back to the palace to turn in for the night.

***

The following morning as Erick was on his way to Elizabeth's room he noticed Myra's loyal servant Gabriel walking out of Myra's room with a hard cold look on his face. He could not make sense of this but didn't think much of it. He continued on towards Elizabeth's room. The same morning as Elizabeth woke she was caught out of surprise; Prince Mark was there sitting on the edge of her bed.

Finding Love

"Oh my Elizabeth said startled.

"I'm sorry to wake you" he said.

Elizabeth looked at Prince Mark. He looked horrible. He looked as if a carriage or something had hit him.

"My prince, please tell me what's wrong?" she asked sitting immediately, worrying about him.

"It's my brother, King George!" Prince Mark started and stopped, he was truly overcome with emotions.

"Is he okay? Has he got worse? What?" She asked.

"No. Not that! He... He passed away awhile ago."

"Oh, Mark I'm am so sorry"

Elizabeth hugged him unexpectedly. Prince Mark was surprised but returned the hug. He needed somebody right now and knew Elizabeth was that person he could count on. Elizabeth pulling back from the hug said "I'm here for you. Whatever you need, I'm here."

Prince looked at Elizabeth for a while and kissed her with more passion that he ever though could happen.

Jessica Lara

Suddenly there was a knock on the door interrupting their special moment.

"Yes" Elizabeth, said frustrated.

"Is Prince Mark in there?" Erick asked.

"Yes?" Prince Mark said.

"Pardon the interruption sir, we need to call the priest and make arrangements for the King's funeral!" Erick stated.

"Right, Of course I'll be down in a bit." Prince Mark said.

Prince Mark kissed Elizabeth once again, and walked to the door.

"Elizabeth, please hurry, I need you beside me?" Prince Mark said.

"Of course I'll be right down, Mark why are we rushing to have the King's funeral. Not that it matters it just it's so fast." Elizabeth said.

"Queen Myra decided that she needs it quickly, too much grieving, first father and now George. And I think the faster we get it done the faster the grief goes away!" Mark said.

"Sorry Mark, the grief will not go away even having a funeral fast! You loved him and he loved

Finding Love

you! You know that! I know that! Erick, Petra, Myra, all of the servants know that! It just doesn't go away like that!" Elizabeth said as she got up and walked over to the door where Mark stood.

"I do believe you, there is so much at stake right now, first my father and I am still searching for the persons behind his death and now my brother. I know that I have been in charge since his illness, but this is almost too much for me. I need some closure and having George's service quickly will help in finalizing some of the issues I have."

"Okay..." Elizabeth gave him a quick 'I understand smile'. I'll get ready quickly!"

"Okay then I'll see you down stairs." He said as he started to leave.

"Mark, when your get down stairs please send Petra up here for me."

"Sure, no problem will do." He said as he closed the door.

***

"You called?" Petra said as she poked her head in

Jessica Lara

Elizabeth's room.

"Yes, can you help me put this on?"

"No problem, that's what I'm here for.

Ironically it didn't take Elizabeth long to get ready. Going downstairs to the breakfast room, Prince Mark and Queen Myra were sitting eating breakfast. Helping herself to a bowl of fruit and eggs and sausage, Elizabeth poured a glass of juice, sitting next to Prince Mark. Elizabeth noticed that the prince was pushing his food around on his plate and not really eating. Queen Myra didn't appear to be suffering from the knowledge of the death of her other stepson. She took the news with the same emotions as the news that bandits had killed her husband.

After breakfast, the ladies walked upstairs to retrieve their wraps and their purses. Arriving at the front of the Palace a carriage was waiting. They walked to the carriage where Prince Mark help them both in and then got in himself. "Mark..." Elizabeth whispered so Myra couldn't hear.

"Yes" Prince Mark replied.

"I don't feel so well!"

Finding Love

"Do you think you can hold up to the end of the funereal?"

Elizabeth was not sure if it was good idea but she knew how much it meant to Prince Mark so she went ahead and said "Of course".

***

The Carriage finally got to the family chapel where everyone was waiting for it to start. Prince Mark got out of the carriage first and then helped Queen Myra and Elizabeth. Moment by moment Elizabeth felt worse. Walking to the church and then to the family gravesite was almost too much for her to bear. Standing listening to the priest seemed endless. Elizabeth felt like she was standing there for hours. Suddenly it started to rain, causing everyone to go inside the church. Prince Mark and Queen Myra stood listening to the expressions of sympathy from the crowd. Elizabeth stood there hoping anytime Prince Mark would turn around and tell her it would be over in a little, but he didn't. Then Elizabeth started to feel dizzy

Jessica Lara

and she walked up to Prince Mark and told him that she felt worse.

"Just hold on it's almost over. Then we can go home. Please Lizy just a little while longer".

"Ma... ark..."

Elizabeth couldn't even finish talking she just fell to the ground unconscious. Prince Mark immediately dropped to the ground next to Elizabeth.

"Elizabeth, Lizy baby please answer me." Prince Mark yelled trying to get Elizabeth conscious.

Picking Elizabeth up Prince Mark ran to the carriage with Queen Myra following and ordered the driver to drive them back to the palace.

Finding Love

Chapter Seven

Arriving at the palace Prince Mark ran Elizabeth inside where he order Petra and Erick to call a doctor, as he ran Elizabeth up to his room and laid her on his bed. Prince Mark sat in a chair next to the bed until the doctor came.

"Doctor Cyrus, thank you for coming, please can you tell me what's wrong with her?" Prince Mark asked impatiently standing up.

"First you'll have to give me time to figure that so I'll have to ask you to leave the room and as soon as I examine her, I'll tell you!" the doctor replied

Jessica Lara

pushing Prince Mark out of the room.

Prince Mark paced back and forth while Erick and Petra watched him. They had never seen him so worried about anyone since his mom passed away. When King George had just got sick, Mark was told that he may not ever recover and he did he would most likely be paralyzed from the neck down, the prince took everything in strive.

After a few minutes Dr. Cyrus came out and closed the door behind him. Mark then turned around and rushed over to him and asked once more.

"What's wrong with her?"

"Well, she's showing signs of poisoning." Dr. Cyrus said.

"What? How could that have happened? That's like unlikely to happen. There's no way you must made a mistake!"

"No I didn't. I'm very sure its poisoning. Look I'm only a doctor. I'm no investigator. So if you need anything else just call. Here's my card." Dr. Cyrus said as he reached into his pocket to pull out a small business card which he handed over to Prince

Finding Love

Mark. "My numbers on there, so just call at anytime if you need me!"

"Look, find a way to get her better or else..." Mark said ignoring Dr. Cyrus handing him the business card.

While Prince Mark went on threatening Doctor Cyrus, the two servants remand silent. Then suddenly Erick seemed to realize something then jumped up and interrupted Prince Mark mid sentence.

"My Prince; I'm sorry to interrupt this mood you are in but the other day I saw Gabriel exiting Myra's room with the cold look on his face. I didn't think much of it until now. Maybe he poisoned Elizabeth. He could of slipped it in her food you know how Myra always gets him to check her food out before serving it to her."

Prince Mark stopped midway through his ranting and looked at him. "How fast could the symptoms start showing?" Mark asked Dr. Cyrus.

"In amount of minutes' even second; it all depends on the poison and the amount used!"

He then looked at the doctor and turned on his

Jessica Lara

heel and walked quickly down the corridor.

"Way to go; now he's probably going to kill him!" Petra said in sarcasm.

"He wouldn't do that!" Erick replied.

Petra just looks at Erick doubtfully.

"Would he?" Erick looked down the hall and didn't see the Prince then took one more glance back at Petra who was still staring at him.

"Oh darn!" Erick mumbled as he and Petra started to run after Prince Mark.

Doctor Cyrus stared after Erick and Petra as they ran after Prince Mark, shakes his head then goes back into the room to check on Elizabeth once more.

As Prince Mark briskly walked down the corridor searching for Gabriel, his steps increased with every moment. He looked left and right, asking any servant if they had seen where Gabriel was. Eventually a servant told Prince Mark that the last time they had seen him, he was out in the stables feeding the horses, and he immediately headed toward the stables. Reach the stables and catching sight of Gabriel incited the prince all the more.

Finding Love

"You bastard" Prince Mark said furiously, grabbing Gabriel by collar lifting him off the ground so that his feet were dangling in thin air.

Before Prince Mark could do anything else, Erick stepped in.

"My Prince, please calm down." Erick said, attempting to stop Mark from throwing his free hand toward Gabriel's face.

Erick held Prince Mark firmly as Mark struggled to get loose, while Gabriel backed away slowly.

"What did I tell you?" said Petra sarcastically.

Erick shot her a glare.

"Ouch that hurt!" Petra said with a sense of humor.

Prince Mark seemed to have calmed down.

"Are you good?" Erick asked.

The Prince jerked away from Erick, gave Gabriel a cold glare and walked out of the stables, growling. Erick and Petra looked at Gabriel, who was rubbing with his neck as the color returned to his face. One more glance and they too left the stables walking after Prince Mark.

"Prince Mark! Prince Mark!" Erick and Petra

Jessica Lara

called after him.

"My Prince, are you okay? I've never seen you like this." Erick said.

Prince stopped, turned to look at Erick and Petra and said.

"Thanks, really. Thanks for your concern and stopping me from punching Gabriel's head off but I'd rather just have some time to myself right now."

"Of course as much time as you need." Erick said.

***

The rest of the night Prince Mark sat next to Elizabeth's bed holding her hand, hoping for her to open her eyes. He sat there for hours until the doctor returned.

"Doctor" Prince Mark said questionably standing still holding Elizabeth's hand.

"Not to worry Prince Mark. I believe we caught the poison in time, at this moment, I'm going to give her the herbs to make her better." Each step of administering the dosage, the doctor explained

Finding Love

what he was doing. Placing the canisters on the bedside table, he scooped some of the ground herbs and mixed it in a glass of water. He walked up to Elizabeth and put his hand under the nape of her neck and lifted her up slightly and tilted the glass against her lips and began to pore. Elizabeth started to cough as the liquid went down.

"You're chocking her," Prince Mark shouted.

"My Prince, there isn't exactly any other way for me to do this." Dr. Cyrus tried to explain.

The Prince looked at the doctor to Elizabeth and then to the glass.

"For goodness sake, give me that!" Prince Mark said as he grabbed the glass from the doctor's hands and put some of the medicine into his mouth. The prince picked up Elizabeth's upper body and sat under her. When he was sure that Elizabeth was in a comfortable position he put his lips against hers and forced the medication down her throat. When he was sure that she swallowed it he drank from the glass again and repeated the action until there was no more medicine in the glass. When he was sure the Elizabeth swallowed the last of the medicine Prince Mark reluctantly pulled his lips away. He looked over at the doctor and saw the doctor staring at him.

"Well that's one way of doing it."

He smiled and looked back at Elizabeth caressing the palm of her hand, feeling its softness. The doctor suddenly felt like he was intruding, picked up his things and walked out the door and closed it softly behind him.

The Prince didn't notice the doctor leaving. He looked down at Elizabeth and whispered softly.

"I will make sure that nothing else will ever happen to you again."

He kissed her on the forehead and accommodated his body so that he was lying beside her. He put his arm under her head so that she was using it as a pillow and he surrounded her with his body, settling in as he also fell fast asleep.

The next morning when Prince Mark woke up Elizabeth was still sleeping. Prince Mark decided to step out for a moment and check on his step-mom. Once Prince Mark left Elizabeth's room walking down the corridor toward his step mom's room.

Finding Love

Reaching the room he reaches out his hand to knock but hesitates when he heard Myra and Gabriel talking.

"Why didn't the poison work?" Queen Myra asked.

"I don't know my Que....en" Gabriel's word drifted as he turned to face the door that now was being blocked by Prince Mark.

"What poison?" Prince Mark asked curiously.

"My dear good morning Gabriel and I were just here talking about how the poison I gave him didn't..." Her sentence began to drift.

"To kill the rats she saw the other day." Gabriel finished.

"Yes the rats but I saw another one. And so did Gabriel!" Myra stated.

"Yes. As I was saying the poison didn't work. There still alive and running around!"

"Really I haven't seen any rats!" Prince Mark said with a smirk.

"Well then. I hope you find your rats." Prince Mark said suspiciously and then turned and began to leave the room.

Jessica Lara

"My Prince," Petra yelled at Prince Mark from the end of the corridor.

"Yes, Petra" Prince Mark responded.

"Elizabeth is awake."

"Well then I'll go see her. Thank you, Petra. Oh and bring her some food she's probably starving."

"Of course, I'll be right up with some food."

Without delay, Prince Mark reached the bedroom door. He raised his fist and softly tapped on the door.

"Come in" Elizabeth said.

Prince Mark slowly opens the door and walks in, closes it behind him and walks up to Elizabeth's bed and sits down in the chair next to it.

"How are you feeling?" Prince Mark asked Elizabeth.

"Oh I feel a little better. What happened to me?" she replied.

"That's good. That's good. It appeared you ingested something that didn't agree with you. Doctor Cyprus said it was poison."

Just as Mark finished speaking, someone knocked on the door. "Yes…" Elizabeth said.

Finding Love

"I have your food miss." Petra said.

"Come in please Petra." Elizabeth told Petra.

Petra opened the door and walked in.

"Here you are Miss Elizabeth" Petra said as she sat the tray of food down on the bed stand.

"Thank you Petra. That will be all." Elizabeth said.

"Of course Miss, just call if you need anything else."

"Thank you Petra."

Petra then exited the room returning to her other duties. Prince Mark set in the chair by the bed and watched Elizabeth eat her lunch. He continued to thank his lucky stars she was okay. Weeks went by and Elizabeth began to gain her strength again. The herbs the doctor had administered allowed her to walk again. It was like she was a new woman. And everyday Prince Mark would walk with her everywhere and they began to get closer.

Chapter Eight

The King of Crunnova had heard of King George's death had decided that he wanted the land of Monrovia its neighboring land. Prince Mark was asked to go to war to satisfy the council's decree for him to become King. Ironically, Prince Mark wasn't ready for war; He didn't possess any of the skills needed to ensure neither he nor his men would not be injured or killed. Every day for two months he would wake up early in the mornings and go practice. For hours he would discuss the art of war with the generals of his Army and plan

Finding Love

strategic armaments with the Navy and his Air Force. He had improved on his hand-to-hand combat skills and his marksmanship. Prince Mark was sure when he was finally equipped to defend his country.

The war was very furious; the council was in charge of the kingdom until the prince returned. Months on months the war raged, many braved men lost their lives defending the country. But the prince was in the middle of the battle. This encouraged the men to fight even harder. They knew that if the prince would put his life on the line for the country then they also would go the limit for Monrovia as well. Each day when the battle would start again, the chant would be heard in the company "long live the King" or "God save the king".

After weeks, months; finally Prince Mark was able to go back home. He wanted to surprise everyone at the palace upon his return. As Prince Mark's carriage passed the village market him spotted Queen Myra at a little market shopping. He couldn't tell what it was but he knew it wouldn't be

Jessica Lara

anything good knowing that Myra never does her shopping for herself.

When Prince Mark arrived at the palace he noticed that Elizabeth was outside by the garden picking flowers with Petra and Erick. He ordered the driver to drop him off by the garden. Not knowing who was in the carriage, the three turned with a questioning glare as the Prince departed from the carriage. Their eyes grew larger and Elizabeth was at a lost as to what to do. She just stood there in amazement suddenly she then dropped the flowers ran over to where Prince Mark was standing and threw her arms around him. Erick and Petra slowly walked behind her allowing the two to reunite with each other.

"Mark, I'm so happy you're back." Elizabeth said as she squeezed Prince Mark with all her might.

"I missed you as well Lizy, it's good to be back!" Prince said with a little laughter in his voice as he hugged Elizabeth back.

The Prince and Elizabeth continued to hug each other forgetting that Erick and Petra was standing near.

Finding Love

"Sorry, it's good to see you guys too!" Prince Mark said finally noticing the two servants standing close to the couple.

"The palace looks wonderful, where's Myra?" asked the prince innocently.

"Oh she said she was going out with Gabriel to get some stuff for the rats in her room"
replied Petra.

"You know I haven't seen one rat lately. Not one! I beginning to believe she is making up the whole thing! I'd like to find a real rat in stick it in her bed and see what will happen!" Erick said.

"Goodness Erick, calm down! Prince Mark is back and this calls for a celebration not terrorizing people" said Petra.

"Yes you are correct Petra, the prince is back and that calls for a celebration. I am quite sure Queen Myra will forget the rats and want to welcome you back with open arms" replied.

"A celebration for what" asked Queen Myra as she walked carefully upon the small group.

"The King is back and Monrovia deserves a celebration, a real king on the throne" Erick said

Jessica Lara sarcastically.

"You know you won't be Queen anymore now that Mark is now becoming King."

"Ha, ha, ha... actually on the contrary, I'm still the Queen and will be until I die or Mark marries. Knowing Mark has no intentions of getting married it appears I will always be Queen of Monrovia.

"Will see about that you..." Erick mumbled under his breath that only Petra could hear him.

"Erick!" Petra whispered holding on to his arm. An attack on the queen could bring great punishment. As the two watched the queens retreating back, both licked their tongues at her. "Don't worry Erick you will have too much to do getting the celebration ready to have the people welcome the king back. It's got to be the greatest ball of all times. Everyone in the kingdom will want to come. Prince Mark the news from the front lines has always been great news concerning your bravery. Your subjects will want very much to let you know how much they appreciate your dedication and sacrifice. Come on Erick we have lots of planning to do. Alert the kitchen, Emily will

Finding Love

love this, preparing a feast to fit a king".

"Are you sure, everyone will be invited to the ball" asked Elizabeth worriedly. "Of course silly, he is the King of Monrovia and his subject deserves to welcome him back" said Erick.

"Oh my, I've got to run a quick errand" said Elizabeth as she ran toward the stables. "Wait Elizabeth, where are you going" asked Petra, "I'll go with you, besides the king told us to watch after you, oops I guess I wasn't suppose to let her know" said Petra holding her hands in front of her mouth. But Elizabeth didn't hear what she had said, she was too intent on running her errand and being back in time to help plan the celebration. Elizabeth ran to the stables mounted the horse the prince gave her before he left, and rode off into the village. Arriving at a familiar house she dismounted and ran to the door.

"Hello, anyone home?" Elizabeth asked.

"Yes, come in" a familiar voice called from inside the house.

"Hi…" Elizabeth said.

"Elizabeth!" Joshua shouted running to the

Jessica Lara

opened door and hugging Elizabeth, taking a step back to take a long good look at her. "What are you doing here? Wow, you look beautiful. Last time I saw the servants' uniform they weren't that great. I guess they've improved!"

"Actually, Mark didn't make me his servant I am his guest, and I get to accompany him to different functions: which is one of the reasons I am here."

"If you are only his guest, then why don't you just leave? Come back I miss you!"

"Sweetie I miss you too. But it's not like that. I can't just leave!"

"Pray tell why can't, you leave; you are not his servant, guest come and go as they please."

"I just can't"

"It hasn't been the same without you Lizy, I need you here, there's no one to talk with and doing all the chores all alone is hard. I am guessing you are really enjoying the life of the rich and famous"

"Joshua, sarcasm doesn't suit you... You know that I miss you remember I am paying the cost for your crime. Yes I do miss you dearly and I wish I could have my best friend with me every day to

Finding Love

help me get through the things I've been going through. But I've have to remain there until the two year period is up, besides I promise that I would and I like being around Prince Mark. He's different and..." Elizabeth stopped. Suddenly she realized that Joshua wasn't listening and nothing she was saying made any difference to Joshua. "Will you talk to me? Will you say something? Please..."

"No! I don't see why I should"

"Joshua, come on. You can't stay mad at me forever..."

"Yes I can" Joshua said cutting the rest of sentence out.

"Joshua?"

"No!"

"Well fine, I just wanted to tell you I do miss you really and everyone in the kingdom is invited to a welcome home celebration for Prince Mark. And I wanted you to, no I need you to be there" Elizabeth waited for an answer. Hearing no reply from Joshua, Elizabeth turned walking to the door looked back once more at Joshua. She quietly

Jessica Lara

closed the door behind her. With sadness that weight very heavy on her shoulders, she rode back to the palace

The sadness was too much for her to bear; she dismounted her horse and dragged herself up the stairs. Prince Mark noticed the disappointment on her face and attempted to question her on the cause. But he was called away to attend the needs of the kingdom. The prince worked far into the night and didn't get the chance to talk with Elizabeth nor to speak with the servants on the arrangement for the celebration. Suddenly the door to the Library burst open and Erick came in yelling

"Prince Mark, your presence is needed at the front door immediately."

"What is it Erick?" Prince Mark asked getting up from his chair.

"You must hurry!" Erick said as he heading back to the front door.

Prince Mark turned to see Elizabeth looking between him and Erick with wide eyes.

The uproar brought all the servants to the front

Finding Love

of the palace, hearing the commotion, Elizabeth started to the front as well.

Standing at the front door as a wounded young man; barely able to stand at attention as he addressed the prince.

"Your majesty!" the young man said as he bowed then stood up straight again. Please forgive the delay in bringing you the news you have been searching for.

"What is it young man?"

"Words finally reached me that you have been searching for the bandits responsible for assault on your father's carriage. I am sorry to say that the facts behind your father's death have been fabricated. Your father did not die as a result of bandits but was bludgeon to death while he was out of his carriage. Bandits do not attack with clubs but with guns. Your guards have been all over the kingdom searching for bandits, and making the villages life very difficult. I would have come sooner but my injuries delayed my arrival".

Prince Marks' face became very pale. He was haunted by the fact his stop-mother had lied about his father's death. "Please take this young man into the kitchen and get him something to eat. Elizabeth, come with me". The Prince barked out order before ascending up the stair, heading for his step-mother's room. Without ceremony he barged into the room

"Mark, please come in, what do I owe the pleasure of your -" Myra said with a smile. She starred at Prince Mark and slowly her smile began to fade. "Mark. What's wrong? Are you okay?"

"Do you want to tell me again just how my father died? It appears that one young man came to the palace to let me know that there is no way that the first story could have happened" Mark said with anger in his voice.

"Son, I am so very sorry, I must confess, it's was all my fault. Your father and I were having a little difference of opinion. I wanted to move back here to the palace so I told him but he didn't care what my desire was and he just jumped out of the carriage. He just jumped.

It's hard for me to admit that your father committed suicide. I thought it be better if I said he

Finding Love

was killed by bandits." Myra said.

Prince Mark starred at her for a while then a calm appearance replaced the angry scowl. "Thank you. I just wanted to know the truth."

Elizabeth's mouth dropped, so many thoughts were running through her mind "What is he thinking? She's lying through her teeth. Mark can't you see that she's lying", she thought.

Prince Mark turned and left the room. Elizabeth ran after him. "Mark, you can't be serious. You actually believe your father committed suicide? I didn't know your father but I give him a more credit than that, after all he had to run a country. You can't really believe that he jumped out of a moving carriage. I can't believe you will take Myra's word over that of the guy downstairs. Besides your brother was ill, I am sure your father would have wanted to see him above all things and to think that he would kill himself versus come here to see you and your brother truly does not make any sense to me."

"Please tell me you don't believe what Myra said?" Elizabeth said with a calmer voice.

Jessica Lara

Prince Mark started to smile with a slit laugh after it. "I don't. But I'm glad you can tell me what's on your mind" the prince said.

Elizabeth starred at him and then just started to laugh as she accompanies him downstairs.

***

After the uproar brought about by the visiting young man, the palace returned to its regular routine. The staff was busy getting things ready for the prince welcome home party. All the neighboring villas had returned acceptance to the celebration. The villagers would have their chance to welcome the prince the following day at a barbeque on the palace grounds. With great expectation the day arrived with much fanfare, the party of the century started with the announcement of many of the royalty Elizabeth met her first night at the palace. Little did Elizabeth know during the celebration parliament would announce Mark as king. The night was magical. Every star in the sky seemed to shine on

Finding Love

Elizabeth and Mark as they greeted the guest and danced. She felt just like Cinderella of the story books. Elizabeth never wanted the night to end because that would be the end of her dreams. The next morning the villagers began to arrive.

"Excuse me. Would you know where I can find Elizabeth?" Joshua asked Erick.

"I remember you, you are her brother, and sure Miss Elizabeth is still in her room. Go up the stairs; turn right, go down to the end of the hallway, turn left, and walk five doors down and you will find her room. She normally leaves her door open so it shouldn't be hard to find" Erick replied.

"Thank you!" Joshua replied as he entered the palace and started up the stairs.

He then went up the stairs, turned right then walked down the hallway until he came to a dead end where he turned left and walked until he found a door open.

Finding the right door, Joshua knocked lightly on the door frame.

"Come in..." Elizabeth said.

Joshua poked his head in to find Elizabeth sitting

Jessica Lara

across the room in front of the mirror. "Hi" Joshua said softly.

Hearing his voice, Elizabeth jumped from her spot on the chair, "Joshua!" I didn't think you were going to come" she said hugging him tightly.

"Of course I had to come. Why wouldn't I? My best friend invited me, so here I am" Joshua told Elizabeth.

"Good! It's going to be great. Come." Elizabeth said as she grabbed his hand and almost running down the stairs to the grounds. Joshua could understand why Elizabeth never wanted to leave the palace, growing up in a small cottage with little made him feel like he was heaven. The village knew that Mark was crowned king the night before and this was their chance to congratulate him on his appointment. The servants had erected a tent with a dance floor so everyone could dance. Mark walked to Elizabeth holding out his hand "May I have this dance, darling?"

Elizabeth looked at him "Yes you may" she said with a great big smile as she placed her hand in his. Everyone watched in silence as Prince Mark and

Finding Love

Elizabeth both walked to the middle of the floor and started to dance. The crowd had all but vanished. Elizabeth was captivated by his eyes and his eyes never left hers.

***

The King arose early in the morning three of his college friends flew into town to help celebrate his crowing. Early morning hunting was the order of the day. "So, how good are you at this?" Mark asked Elise.

"Average" Ellis mumbled.

"What are you kidding? He's great!" said Alton Ellis's faithful servant.

"Thank you Alton! So how good are you?"

"I really don't know I guess will find out." Mark said with a laugh.

The King, Ellis and Alton all went into the woods to start to hunt. After hours of nothing they decided to pack up and head back. Out of nowhere an arrow pierced the King's shoulders. Ellis grabbed his friend and rode with haste back to the palace. Upon seeing their arrival, "oh my; gosh what happened?' Elizabeth yelled as she ran to the horse and riders.

"It appears that some dumb hunter mistook Mark for a deer. No madam let me get him. Just please call a doctor." Ellis said as he got off his horse and grabbed Mark.

Elizabeth ran inside and ordered Petra to call the doctor as she ran after Ellis and directed him to Mark's room. A light tap on the door and Elizabeth opened the door for the doctor.

"Doctor Cyrus, thank you for coming!" Elizabeth said.

It's always a pleasure to come to the palace, just wish it isn't for someone being sick, what do we have here?" Doctor Cyrus asked.

"Well we were out..." Ellis started.

"He was shot" Elizabeth interrupted.

"Yeah that!" Ellis said.

"My, my, now if you two will just step outside I can see the extent of his injury and let you know my prognosis." Doctor Cyrus told Elizabeth and Ellis.

Finding Love

"No! I'm staying right here." Elizabeth snapped back.

"Sorry Miss Elizabeth you may get in my way and I need to be clear in what to do next. Elizabeth didn't move, so Doctor Cyrus went ahead and started to clean the area around the Mark's shoulder, placing his hands against his cheats, grabbed the arrow and pulled. Elizabeth stated to gag, she felt sick. She immediately ran out the room. Ellis and Doctor Cyrus both looked at the door, smiled and continued to administer first aid to the King.

"I told her…" Doctor Cyrus said with a smile.

About five minutes later Doctor Cyrus and Ellis exited the room, Elizabeth immediately jumped from her chair and said "how is he doing, can I see him now"?

"The King will be alright, he will need a lot of rest but he will be back to his old self in about a week or two" Doctor Cyrus said.

"Thank God what a relief" Elizabeth interrupted.

"Thank you so much Doctor Cyrus," Elizabeth said giving the doctor a quick hug and walking into the

Jessica Lara

King's room. Sitting in the very chair Mark sat while she was sick, she took up the vigilance in taking care of the King. She wiped his brow with a damp cloth. She sat all night beside his bed never leaving his side. With every slight movement, she would sit up straight and watch him very carefully. She started to fall asleep when she was jerked awake and was staring in the eyes of the King.

"Oh, I'm sorry to wake you." Elizabeth stated.

"No, I was already awake" he replied.

Doctor Cyrus had left additional dressings and some ointment to put on the Kings wound. Elizabeth started to redress his shoulder. "Ouch, that hurts" the King complained.

"Oh Mark stop being such a baby, we have to keep this dry and clean" Elizabeth remarked

"Baby, I'm your baby" King said with a smile.

Mark then sat back without saying a word allowing Elizabeth to redress his wound.

"Doctor Cyrus said you have to remain in bed for a week or two. Do you think you can do that"?

"Elizabeth, me staying still and quiet is not going to happen, someone shot me with a darn arrow

Finding Love

and I need to find out whom".

"You will have time for that when you get better, if you want your wound to get worse and hurt ten times as much as it does now then go ahead go and get up and start to do whatever you want. And when it hurts like hell and it stars to bleed a lot then don't come to me crying." Elizabeth said pointing her hand toward the door but kept her eyes focused on Mark as he looked back and forth a few times before settling his eyes back on Elizabeth.

Mark just stared at Elizabeth not knowing what to say, he didn't say anything. She challenged him, standing up for what she knows to be right. He admired that quality in her. She was unique and suddenly he can't imagine his life without her being a part of it.

Following the doctor's order and Elizabeth's administration he stayed in bed. Within two week's Mark started to feel better. Doctor Cyrus would occasionally come and visit to make sure that the wound was not infected. From his bed he would tend to the affairs of his kingdom without missing a beat. Within two months he was better than ever.

Almost daily very early in the morning, the king would take his prize stallion and ride for exercise. Myra startled him, never had she gotten up early enough to witness his ride. "Are you alright Mother? I don't ever remember you being up this early."

"I miss you and we need to talk. It's been a long time since we had a mother-son conversation. Please sit with me a few minutes before your ride" the queen replied. "Mark, I must speak to you concerning that little pleasant girl. Everyone in the kingdom is talking. It doesn't look good having her here under our roof. How long will she to be here"?

When Elizabeth woke up early after getting dressed she started down stairs but stopped having heard her name mentioned by the Queen. Sitting on the stairs she continued to listening on what was being said.

"I am not sure what you are getting at Mother; it's not a big deal."

Finding Love

"Mark it is a big deal, as I said the whole kingdom is talking. She is not our kind, she don't belong in the palace. She has no business being here and keeping her as your play thing is one thing but keeping her in the palace does not look good. You have to consider what other nations will think of this arrangement. Plus after you finish playing with her she will suffer going back to that simple life she once loved living. Did you ever notice that little cottage she lived in, it's a pig sty". Myra continued belittling Elizabeth.

"Again, Mother I don't know what you are talking about, Lizy is not my play thing, she is my guest here and you will have to respect my decisions. I don't care what the other nations are thinking, I cannot control their thought patterns, but I will control my life and that of Lizy's."

"Son, I know that you like this little diversion in your life, but" – Myra started saying

"Like her? Who said I liked her!" Mark said trying to lead Myra in a different direction.

Elizabeth not wanting to hear any more ran upstairs to her room large tears filling her eyes.

Jessica Lara

She knew that in the months she has been in the palace, she was more than in love with the king. Her heart was breaking into pieces. She knew she had to get away but she was so very torn, she didn't want to leave his presence. Everyday seeing him made her heart skip a beat. When he smiled her way it totally illuminates her very being. "How can I leave" she reasoned with herself, but she knew she couldn't stay for the very same reasons she wanted to stay.

The conversation between the King and Queen Myra continued "Son its time that you think about getting married. The by-laws of this kingdom decree you will have to marry royalty."

Eavesdropping in on the conversation "that's not true, my goodness she is such a liar" Petra whispered under her breath.

"Mother, I believe you are mistaken, when did that rule become law?"

"Mark, the kingdom of Monrovia has had that on the books for a long time. Why do think your father married me?"

"Mother I am thinking Father was a very lonely

Finding Love

old man you were beautiful in your day and your family had money" the King replied.

"Son, let's be serious you can't, marry her. In fact I absolutely forbid you to even thinking of marrying her. Do you realize that you will have to renounce your throne and I really doubt you would want to give it up everything for a peasant girl? Would you?"

Not wanting to answer his step-mother, the king finally replied "most definitely not."

"Thank goodness, I am so glad we had this little chat" the Queen replied. Mark feeling dismissed arose from the couch and proceeded to the stables. He knew what he wanted and right now the fresh air would do him good. Since the conversation was over, Petra left her hiding place to finish her chores for the day.

***

The reminder of the month passed with little incident. Mark was called to the far region to examine the borders against insurgents. Several

Jessica Lara

villages were being raided. He knew that he had to hire more guards to protect the outer areas. During his absence the palace was strangely quiet and a dreary place. Elizabeth was at a lost at what to do. She wished with everything in her that he would have asked her to accompany him as he tour the country side. A carriage ride, she thought of the romantic possibility. She even envisioned him falling in love with her. The Queen had tried to be a gracious hostess but there was always something lying beneath her display of welcome. She would always make Elizabeth feel like an unwanted guest. Conversation was very strained. So most of her days involved walks in the garden and sitting in the gazebo remembering their dance and their first kiss. Even the smell of the rain reminded her of the king. She would almost hear his laughter in the halls and feel his eyes on her when she set to dine. Elizabeth knew that there was no way she could ever win the Queen over, no matter how well dressed or how refine she could walk or talk. In the eyes of the Queen she wasn't royalty and would never be good enough for the King. Plus each day

Finding Love

she could remember hearing the King saying he didn't like Elizabeth and the Queen reminding him of the royal decree that he must marry royalty.

Word reached the palace that the King was on his way home. Again the servants flew into a frenzy getting the palace ready for his return. Elizabeth was so excited she couldn't eat and even the Queen's displeasure didn't find its mark on her enthusiasm. Every morning she woke up singing, the sun was brighter and the flowers smelled sweeter. Her walks were very close to the palace, she didn't want to miss his arrival. Upon returning to the palace after one of her daily walks, a letter was sitting on her bed. She recognized the handwriting of Doctor Cyrus.

> Ms Elizabeth Clarisse Bailly,
>
> I am sorry to inform you that your brother is gravely ill. It appears he has contracted Swine Influenza. I am afraid in his weaken condition this virus will prove to be very taxing on him. Since you are his only friend and almost sister, he has named

Jessica Lara

> you as next of kin. It also appears he contracted this disease some time ago and with no insurance Joshua did not seek medical attention; early treatment would have eliminated the toll the flue is taking on his body. I must prepare you for the worst. I will remain with him until I can see a change one way or the other.
>
> Doctor Cyrus

After reading the doctor's note, Elizabeth quickly ran down the stairs and mounted her horse. She rode like the very devil was after her. Reaching the cottage, she jumped off the horse almost as soon as she stopped. No one at the palace noticed her departure. When the King arrived all the servants met him at the door, even Queen Myra was present to witness his arrival. One person was missing and she was the only one the King was looking for. "Petra, please go and see if Elizabeth is in her room and tell her I need to see her in the Library." Petra flew back down the stairs and ran into the library, "your majesty, she is not in her

Finding Love

room; I found this letter on the floor". After reading the note from the doctor, Mark then threw the letter down on his desk and ran out to the stables. He mounted his horse and rode bare back. When Elizabeth reached the cottage she ran inside looking for Joshua and Doctor Cyrus. "How is he doctor" she asked. I am afraid my dear he is worse than I feared. He has all the symptoms; fever, coughing, chills, diarrhea and vomiting. If I can't control the last two I am afraid we may lose him" replied the doctor. When the King reached the cottage, Elizabeth was nowhere to be seen. The doctor was alone with Joshua, "where is Elizabeth" he demanded of the doctor. "I am not sure, she ran out the door a few seconds ago, she couldn't have gone far. She was very upset at the news of her friend". Heading out the door he looked to the left then to the right and spotted her standing looking out over the ocean. She looked very small standing there her back to the King. Mark knew the news of Joshua was hitting her hard, his heart felt her pain. Coming up behind her, he softly spoke her name, "Elizabeth will you be alright" he asked.

Jessica Lara

"I'm not sure, if I lose Joshua, I have lost everything. Mark I don't know what I will do without him" she turned and fell in the Kings' arms in tears.

"Does he mean that much too you" the King asked in a very hurt tone. He remembered she said that she would die for Joshua.

"Yes, he does mean that much to me. Joshua's my best friend."

"Best friends? You mean you are in love with him?"

"No I am not in love with Joshua, I love him. He has been my only and best friend since I can remember. He has always been there for me. After our parents died, we sort of start taking care of each other. We are all that we have"

"Now I can't see him, the doctor said he is highly contagious and he is so sick I may never see him again." Elizabeth started to cry more. "Oh Mark he is dying, what am I going to do?"

"Elizabeth don't think that way, you have got to be brave. Doctor Cyrus is the best doctor in town and Joshua is a strong young man. I promise he

Finding Love

will pull through. He has you in his corner.

Looking in the King's eyes, Elizabeth suddenly believed what he said; she laid her head on his shoulder and looked out on the ocean once more.

"You know I believe you Mark, thank you" Elizabeth said never raising her head, just feeling the warmth of his body and relishing in his embrace. The doctor convinced Elizabeth that she should go back to the palace with the King there was nothing she could do for Joshua that night. Beside he and the nurse will be there and they had everything under control. He would let her know as soon as he had more information concerning Joshua's condition.

The next morning the King asked Elizabeth to come and ride with him. He promised to send someone to check on Joshua. The day was perfect in her mind. The sun was high in the sky and a light breeze kept them cool as they rode far from the palace. The King had a picnic lunch already prepared and waiting for them when they arrived at this little cove he found when he was a boy. Soon the King had convinced Elizabeth to take off her shoes so they could walk along the water edge. They ran and splashed each other and laughed until the sun began to set. "Elizabeth we must return home, it's getting dark and I still have a few papers to go over before I go to congress tomorrow". Returning to the palace, the King went to his library and remained there late into the night. Elizabeth sitting before her mirror brushing her hair and could not get the beauty of the day out of her mind. So intent on dreaming about the King she did not hear the noise behind her until it was too late. A handkerchief was placed over her nose and mouth and she lost consciousness.

The next morning when Petra went to wake Elizabeth for breakfast, she noticed Elizabeth wasn't in her room, her bed wasn't slept in, and the window was wide open. Petra immediately ran down stairs to tell the King.

"Your highness." Petra yelled as she ran down stairs.

"Elizabeth is missing sire she is not in the palace. Her bed hasn't been slept in and there is something not right about the condition of her room."

Finding Love

"Maybe she just left earlier to get some air or to go check on Joshua. Erick, Aston go check the stables to see if her horse is missing. And the rest of you check the palace grounds and see if she went for a walk. Check the gazebo to see if she's there. Report back here immediately." King Mark ordered the staff. He then began to pace back and forth. While Erick was checking the stables Aston ran out to the gazebo to see if she was sitting. When Erick reached the stables Erick started to count the horses and then noticed none were missing. Erick then recounted two more times hoping that he had miscounted. Aston reached the gazebo, no Elizabeth. He then searched the grounds she was nowhere to be found. Each of the servant returned stating they could not find Elizabeth anywhere. The King ordered the guard to search every house, cottages, and caves. His exact words were to leave no stone unturned but at the end of the day there was still no sign of Elizabeth. Days went by and still no sign of Elizabeth.

One morning while Erick went to go check on the King, Petra noticed an envelope that had been

Jessica Lara

slipped under the door. It was address to Mark.

Mark,

You have no rights to the throne. It is rightfully mine. If you wish to see this lovely creature again, you will renounce yourself and announce me as King of Monrovia. Your father did not have the right to the throne. My father should have been crowned king. I promise not to harm Elizabeth, she is a delightful child. I have tried without success in getting rid of you and your brother. George was easy, the poison worked, it was slow and painful as I had hoped, I missed you with the arrow, but I notice how much she means to you. If you want her then you know what to do. If you agree with these conditions, leave a note at pier 6. Be careful; remember I have the woman you love. Someone will retrieve the note and I will meet you and only you to sign over the throne. Absolutely no guards you will be watched.

Finding Love

> The rightful king,
>
> Paul

Mark stood staring at the letter.

"Your majesty, is everything alright, is it news about Elizabeth?" Petra asked.

"My cousin Paul has her. He wants to trade her for the crown. It appears it was he that attempted to kill me when we were out hunting.

When we were little about thirteen years old, Father remarried Myra, Paul heard that he was moving out of the palace and leaving George the crown and I was in line for the throne. Paul also was the reason for George's illness and believed he wouldn't be king long. He knew there were no other siblings in line for the throne he asked if anything happened to me when I was King if he could he be crown king of Monrovia. Unfortunately, he will never be able to assume the crown nor the throne. Paul is a harden criminal and the only reason he has not been executed is he escaped and hadn't been heard from. Now he has

Jessica Lara

Elizabeth and wants to trade her life for the throne."

"Your Majesty, we can trick Paul into coming to the palace and the guards can arrest him. He is obviously insane, if he thinks that just signing papers can make him king with all that is against him. All we have to do is deliver the note saying you will renounce the throne after he brings Elizabeth back. The papers will be in the office for him to sign and the council will have to make the announcement the following day" Erick explained.

"That sounds almost too good to be true, but as you said, Paul is obviously insane, he just may fall for it. Alert the guards. Make sure everyone remains out of sight until we know that Elizabeth is safe and Paul is in the palace."

Paul,

You leave me no choice. You are correct I do love Elizabeth and desire that nothing happens to her. Monrovia is yours. Tomorrow evening, come to the library, the papers will be ready for your signature. I have ordered the guards to stand down you will have an unrestricted passage to the

Finding Love

> palace. A letter has been sent to the council alerting my decision to denounce the throne. If anything happens to Elizabeth all conditions are voided.
>
> Mark

One of the King's men delivered the note to the pier. The following evening, the palace appeared to be deserted. No guards were in sight. Paul boldly walked to the front door and entered with Elizabeth in tow. She was breathing hard, she was all bruised, her dress was all dirty and torn; her hair was all tangled and falling out of the bun. Her hands were tied in front of with rope that Paul used to pull her behind him. When he arrived at the library, Mark was sitting behind the desk.

"I hope you feel comfortable, this will be the last time you sit behind my desk" Paul said with a sneer.

"Paul, how wonderful it is to see you again. As you can notice, the papers are drawn up and are ready for your signature" the King said

Jessica Lara sarcastically.

Releasing his hold on Elizabeth, Paul quickly walked around the desk to sit in his place of honor. "Now" said the King. Immediately the guard jumped out from behind the heavy curtains and place Paul under arrest.

"You tricked me" Paul was crying angrily. He attempted to elude the guard in order to get to the King but they had a very tight hold on him. The King wasn't paying any attention to Paul and his ravings. His eyes were fastened on Elizabeth. He knelt beside her and started untying the rope.

"I'm so sorry this happened to you, are you alright" the King said, raising her up with him to her feet. The need to embrace her was overwhelming.

"Mark I was so frighten, but I knew you would find me. He is a very strange man, he just kept repeating, long live King Paul. Is that his name?" Elizabeth said.

"Don't worry he will never bother us again. Come let's get you cleaned up. Petra, take Elizabeth upstairs and let her get a hot bath". Ringing the bell he ordered Emily to fix a tray and

Finding Love
take it up to Elizabeth's room.

***

Sleep eluded Elizabeth. She looks at her clock it was three-fifteen in the morning. Every time she drifted off to sleep, she would wake with a start. She groans and rolls out of bed. She only had few hours of trouble sleep. So she stopped trying. Walking to the window and looking up.

"Oh, my" she whispered. The night was magical, tiptoeing downstairs she walked out into the garden. "It's so beautiful" She whispered. There more stars then she had ever seen and the moon - the moon looked especially close. She was mesmerized. Out of nowhere there were three men circling her.

"What do you want, and why are you here" she asked frighten.

"Little girls shouldn't be out at night, with a slip of lace on" one of the men said leeringly. Another grabbed her, trying to kiss her. She quickly opened her mouth and clamp down as hard as she could.

Jessica Lara

He yelled and started to strike her. "You just bit me, you little -"

She squeezed her eyes shut and braced herself for the pain. But instead she suddenly felt cool air. Opening her eyes she witness Mark single-handedly taking on all three men. His hand to hand combat training testified to his quickness and accuracy when he delivered the blows.

"The only reason I'm not going to kill you is because I know I'll frighten her." His voice filled with so much venom and hate. "I'll have you know I take care of what's mine. You have two minutes for vacate these grounds and never darken this area again. I swear to God if you ever come near the palace or her again, I will kill you slowly and painfully." Hearing his threat, they wasted no time running.

"Elizabeth, trouble seems to follow you everywhere." He whispered as he took a few steps closer. There was silence between them and he pulled her into his arms. She buried herself into his chest and relaxed herself completely against him. Mark then buried his face into her hair and inhaled.

Finding Love

He then picked Elizabeth up and began walking toward the palace. Elizabeth kept herself buried against him.

"I promise to keep you safe." He whispered to her as they enter the palace.

Elizabeth expected the King take her back to her room but instead he walked past her door. Elizabeth looked up at him.

"What are you doing?" She asked.

He looked down at Elizabeth. "You're staying with me tonight" he replied as he entered his room. "You won't get in to any more trouble if your here". As he undressed he said "don't worry, I'll stay on my side of the bed." Laughing he pulled her into his chest.

"You will have to stay on my side." He whispered into her ear.

Falling asleep, Elizabeth said "Mark, don't leave me".

Kissing her forehead, Mark whispered "never."

***

Jessica Lara

He was awake for about fifteen minutes just watching her sleep. The way her breast would raise up and down and the slight opening of her mouth was intoxicating. "Wake up." Mark whispered into Elizabeth's ear. Elizabeth opened her eyes slowly and looked over at Mark.

"Good morning, how did you sleep?" he asked with a smile.

"Hi, I really don't remember falling asleep. I hope I didn't snore or do something gross in my sleep." Elizabeth said back with a smile.

"I will never tell. Come on we have to get up. Breakfast will be ready soon" Mark said. They stared at each other for a while in silence. Elizabeth reaches up and runs her fingers through his dark curls.

"Well we better get up. We have a big day ahead of us." Mark said jumping out of bed. Elizabeth nodded, taking one more stretch, climbed out of bed and heading out the room. One last look at the King, Elizabeth hated the thought of being away from him for the few minutes it would take for her to shower and dress for breakfast.

Finding Love

"Elizabeth?" Mark said.

"Yes my King"

"Nothing, I will see you downstairs" Mark kissed her on the forehead yet again and turned back into his room.

Elizabeth hasten to her room and took a quick shower, she dressed with care. It was important to let Mark see her at her best. She was surprise to see him standing at the foot of the stairs. The sight of him took her breath away, but she smiled, reaching to take his out stretched hand. Breakfast was full of small talk, laughter and secret looks. Queen Myra was noticeably upset with the display of emotions and grunted as she left the table. After breakfast, the duties of the kingdom called Mark to his office. Elizabeth took one of her walks and noticed that Erick was following her, she didn't mind his presence, and in fact she welcomed him to being close.

Later Mark came looking for her, "Elizabeth, I hate to ask you this, but I need you to accompany me to Paul's execution. Do you think you are up to it?" "Mark I will be with you and I can survive anything". Arriving at the gallows Elizabeth started to shiver. Watching this form of punishment was too barbaric, looking over at Mark she noticed the King didn't look as if he was enjoying this capital punishment either. As the verdict was read and the executioner took his place, Elizabeth braced herself for the worst. Mark couldn't believe he was about to do this but the law of the land must be enforced. After a few minutes all the criminals and Paul were escorted out, they turned to face the court. The sentence was pronounced and the executioner pulled the level.

"Let's go home..." Mark said.

Elizabeth looked at Mark and nodded slowly as they got up and exited the gallows. On the way back to the Palace Mark noticed Elizabeth was awfully quiet.

"What's bothering you Elizabeth" Mark asked her.

"Nothing really", she said looking out the window.

"You know, you're a bad liar!" Mark said sitting back with his eyes closed.

Finding Love

Elizabeth closed her eyes for awhile, after a moment she returned to staring out the window. Watching her, Mark knew something was bothering her, yet she wouldn't tell him. When they returned to the palace, Mark took Elizabeth's hand, pulling her into the lounge. Sitting on the sofa, he sat her in his lap. "Elizabeth, you must tell me what's bothering you."

"If I tell you, you will hate me!" Elizabeth answered quietly.

"Lizy, hate isn't an emotion I feel for you. You have to tell me so we can move forward." Elizabeth looked deep into Mark's eyes, trying to read his emotions. Patiently Mark waited for her to tell him what was bothering her. Tears threaten to fall, Mark wiped them away.

"Please tell me" Mark said with sympathy.

"When I was a teenager my parents were killed, the people responsible were caught and executed. Watching Paul's death brought it all back to me. I was so torn, watching it caused such pain; I hated the bandits that caused my parents death and wanted them to suffer so much. It didn't bring my parents back so I felt guilty. I am sorry I disappointed you."

"Sweetheart you can't ever disappoint me. I am so sorry I had you go with me. Paul's execution was a little too much for me as well. As King I must enforce the law though. If I had pardoned him, it wouldn't have set favorable emotions in the kingdom. I will try not to ever involve you in something like that again." Mark said as he tightened his hold.

***

In keeping with his duties as the king, Mark pulled several law books and did his studies. He spent hours and hours until he went through every book on laws. He was looking more for the law that the Queen had told him about his inability to marry a non-royal person. Ironically there was no law such as that on the books but then he stumbled onto something that piqued his curiosity. Stuff in an old law book was his father's marriage certificate to Myra. Along with this certificate was

Finding Love

Myra's birth certification proving she wasn't royalty but a peasant. The very thing she accused Elizabeth of being. Mark was livid; morning wouldn't come fast enough so he could present this evidence to Myra. Immediately after breakfast, he saw the Queen sitting near the atrium. "Mother"

"Yes?" Myra asked as she took another sip of her tea.

"I decided to study a little last night." Mark said sitting near the Queen.

"That's good to know Son, what did you learn?" as she takes another sip of her tea.

"Laws..."

Myra coughed "you were studying laws, how interesting. Did you find everything you needed?"

"Yes. I found out that you lied."

"Lied?"

"Yes Mother. There isn't a law that says I can't marry someone that isn't royalty. And if I understand correctly you were not born into royalty either."

"Where did you hear that?"

Jessica Lara

"This!"

Laying the two documents on the table in front of Myra, Mark waited for her to justify the reasons for the lie she told.

"Now you know the truth, I wasn't royalty"

"What I am trying to understand is why did you lie to me?"

"If you must know, it's because I don't like that peasant girl; that's why."

"I need you to know, it is not about you. It's about me and Elizabeth."

***

Two years seem to have flown by. Elizabeth stood in the room she had come to call hers. She looked around and wonders how she will be able to reestablish herself back into the cottage. Joshua was doing wonderful, getting over the flu had strapped his strength but the King had fulfilled his promise to have someone check on Joshua. The servants also took care of the garden and the chickens. The cottage was flourishing and they

Finding Love

were able to stand on its own. With reservations she started packing what little she had brought with her. She was aware that the grand garments the King had provided for her while she was in the palace would not fit in the scene of the cottage. "Where will I be able to wear this" Elizabeth said out loud

"What are you doing?" Mark said, standing in her door.

Watching him standing there with a question look, brought about new pains in her heart. "My required two years are finished. It's hard to believe that I have been here two years. I don't have any reason for remaining here." Sitting down on the bed, tears filled her eyes. She refused to look at Mark. It worried her that he wanted her to leave realizing her sentence was up. Quietly he walked further in the room.

"Elizabeth" he said, lifting her head so she could see him. "I have known that your two years were up. I was hoping you had forgotten the stipulations placed on you. Are you ready to go?"

Jessica Lara

"Mark, it isn't about what I want. You are the one that set the conditions. I am going by your rules. What is it that you desire my King"?

"Lizy I don't want you to leave!"

Standing up finally, she reaches out to touch his face. "Then don't make me leave."

Sudden passion touched his heart, so much so he pressed him lips against hers. Caressing her back he began kissing her neck, trading her neck for her jaw line and then back to her lips. He lifted his mouth for a second to say "never."

Joy filled her heart and all she could do was smile.

"Elizabeth, my kingdom is vast; I have servants in several different houses. All are subject to everything I say. Today my love, I have something to ask of you."

"Yes?"

With promo and ceremony he lowered himself to the floor.

"I love you and want you to be my queen." In his breast pocket was a large jewelry box. "This ring belongs to my mother, the first queen. It has

Finding Love

always been her wish that I present this to the woman I love. I love you Elizabeth Clarisse Bailly. Will you marry me?"

"But Mark, I thought there was a rule on the books saying you are not allowed to marry a peasant woman" She said.

"So where did you get that piece of information"?

"I am sorry; I overheard Queen Myra and you talking the other day. You told her you didn't like me".

"I lied to her that day, I was confused about my feelings, but now I realize it was more then like, I know that I love you with everything that is in me".

"I love you more than life itself. And yes my love I will marry you and reign as your queen."

Jessica Lara

Chapter Nine

Elizabeth woke with a slight jerk. Her eyes flew open to see she was in Mark's arms in their bed. She pinched herself mentally. It's hard to believe they have been married for six months. The wedding ceremony was more than she could have hoped for. Every villager came to the palace to witness their special day. Joshua was so handsome when he stood next to her as the father of the bride. Her only regret was her parents could not witness their daughter becoming the wife of a wonderful man. She smiled at her husband and snuggled down again in Marks arms and went back

Finding Love

to sleep. The next morning Mark woke up first. He watched his wife sleep and wondered how he could be so lucky. He planted a small kiss on her lips. Realizing the kiss wasn't enough; he smiled and leaned in to kiss her fully. Totally awake, Elizabeth returned the kiss with vigor.

"Good morning my love" Mark said.

"Good morning my husband, are you ready for breakfast" Elizabeth responded.

"I rather have more of you, but we do have a very busy day. It's about time for me to return running the country. What do you have planned for today?"

"Oh I didn't know." Elizabeth said sarcastically with a big grin.

Mark began to laugh as he sat up and headed toward the door. Then he paused and looked back at Elizabeth. "Are you coming wife?"

Elizabeth grinned walked over to Mark, "yes, let's go husband" she said as she grabbed his hand and headed downstairs. They acted like two young kids in love. Elizabeth would feed him a little before feeding herself. Breakfast was sweeter and was

Jessica Lara

over too soon. "Before you go to your office, let's run to the market" Elizabeth suggested.

"So may I ask why we came?" Mark asked as they where waking through the market.

"I just wanted spend one more day with you before you settle down."

"Okay. I guess this is a nice place. But why here?"

"I don't know where else do you suggest?"

"Well there's always the beach you know? And places I think you would love."

"On our next escape day, you can take me to one of your choosing. Although having your guards around all the time isn't much of an escape" Elizabeth said looking behind her at the two armed guards always with the king.

The servants were purchasing fresh vegetables and supplies for the palace. The hustle and bustle of the market was disturbed by a very faint sound coming from her right. Elizabeth stopped walking looking to where the sound was coming from. Near to where she was standing, in a dark alley a whimper. "Did you hear that" she asked Mark. Following the sound, Elizabeth found a small, blond

Finding Love

hair child, lying among the trash crying. Elizabeth kneeled down next to the young child. "Are you alright, sweetheart" she asked. At first the child didn't answer the queen. "Please don't be afraid, I promise not to hurt you. What is your name?" Elizabeth asked.

Keeping her eye adverted, the child shook her head, "I don't know"

Elizabeth's mouth opened slightly. Looking at her husband, "honey we have to do something, It's obvious she doesn't have a family".

The King looked at his wife and then at the little street urchin, "she is so very small, I guess she won't eat much. Are you sure you want to do this? There are orphanages in the village we can take her to".

"Mark no, those places are so over-crowded, she needs us. Please sweetheart, we have plenty of room". Her voice trails as she begins to notice the scars on her arms.

"Oh my…" she whispered. She then got down on her knees so she was eye level to the young girl.

Jessica Lara

"What happened sweetie, did you fall and hurt yourself?" The little girl only shook her head no. Elizabeth gingerly reached out to take the little girl in her arms. Looking first very unsure, the little girl slowly untangled herself from the trash heap and allowed the queen to embrace her. "So what do you want as your name?"

The little girl stared at Elizabeth before answering "I want to be called Aubrey"

"What a pretty name. Where'd you get it?" Elizabeth asked curiously.

"It's my mother's name."

Elizabeth asked "where is your mother?"

"She's in heaven with Daddy." The little girl said as a little tear ran down her cheek.

Wiping her tears, Elizabeth softly said "not to worry sweetheart, we will be your mommy and daddy now."

Laying her head on Elizabeth's shoulder as the King said, "Let's go home, she needs a good bath and food I am sure she is quite hungry".

Finding Love

Chapter Ten

"Petra where's Aubrey?" Elizabeth asked.

"She's outside playing with Emily. They are having tea" Petra responded.

"Thank you. It's time to plan her birthday party". It's hard to believe we have been a family for a year. I must talk with the king to see who we want to invite. I'm still not into all this royalty stuff. Maybe I can talk to Queen Myra she's royalty and know who to invite to little girls' parties". Elizabeth explains to Petra.

Jessica Lara

"Your highness, one thing about the king, he isn't about all the pomp and ceremony. You know the cooks, Erick, the butlers, all the maids, me and you, the king and even Queen Myra. It's amazing how she has changed since you two have become part of the family."

"Thank you Petra, again your sensible nature has won out. Of course we shall have a family party, Myra will love having a party" Elizabeth said. "When Emily finished playing with Aubrey have her come see me. I need to see what we will have to eat. Also, we have to let Queen Myra have her inputs, you are right; she has come to love Aubrey as much as I do". While you go to the market and get some decorations, I will go out to the atrium and sip tea with the princess. Mark will be so happy when he returns. Good, the plans are in work. Well I am going to go outside and sip up some imaginary tea!"

As she reached the door to the atrium, Elizabeth stopped short. Aubrey's tea table was upset; all the cups and saucers were on the floor. Emily had

Finding Love

gone back in the kitchen getting more cookies, and Aubrey was nowhere to be seen.

"Aubrey" Elizabeth called very calmly at first. "Aubrey, Baby. Aubrey, answer me baby! It's mommy." At that moment, panic set in. Running back into the palace, she calls Petra and Emily, "I can't find Aubrey, please help me find her".

Within seconds, all the staff was galvanized to search of the princess. "Aubrey!" "Aubrey!" "Aubrey!" was being yelled from every area of both inside the palace and outside.

"Aubrey! Aubrey! My baby where are you?" Elizabeth screamed running through the garden coming to the maze, stopping long enough to get her bearing before entering the maze. Elizabeth came out on the opposite side of the maze but still no Aubrey. The tears came quicker and more abundantly. Casting a quick glance at the woods, Elizabeth questioned the staff "has anyone checked the woods yet?"

"No. I didn't think it was necessary Aubrey is terrified of the woods"

Jessica Lara

"I don't care if you think it's unnecessary. I don't care if you think the places that Aubrey hates or she's afraid of wouldn't be somewhere she'd be. I want every section of this palace searched. Every square foot searched!" Elizabeth said as she looked at each member of the staff. "I do mean every square inch of this place and the woods searched" she emphasized.

Elizabeth turned back to face the woods. Mark wasn't here to save her this time. She had more at stake than herself this time, taking a deep breath she started walking toward the woods. The faint sound of an approaching carriage caused her to stop.

"Mark!" Elizabeth whispered.

Stepping out of the carriage Marks looks up at the palace and smiled. He was so happy to be home with his family, looking toward Elizabeth. The tears in her eyes and the desperate look on her face caused his heart to miss a beat. "Elizabeth, tell me, what's wrong? Totally giving in to the tears she attempted to tell Mark Aubrey was missing. The tension was too much, she started to fall but

Finding Love

he catches her and pulled her into his chest. "Aubrey... Aubrey's gone, she's missing." She said between gasps of air. Looking into her face, "look at me!" he said, but she didn't move. "Look at me Elizabeth!" He said as he shook her slightly. "I promise you, we're going to find her!"

Elizabeth looked onto his face then back to his eyes. He looked so serious.

"Yes sweetie, we will so let's go find her!"

He smiled for a matter of two seconds before getting serious once more and reaching out for her hands.

"Yes, let's go find her" Elizabeth smiled as they faced the forest together.

"A ubrey!" They all yelled as they walked through the forest together.

The sun began to set, with the approaching evening the coolness was setting in. A small lump laid in their path. It was one of Aubrey's dolls. Elizabeth knew they were on the right track. "Aubrey, Aubrey, Aubrey" she calls to the top of her voice. "Aubrey, Aubrey". They had cleared the forest and found themselves at the clearing

Jessica Lara

overlooking the ocean. Her tiny form was standing near the edge, her back to the forest. Aubrey stood very still, almost too still.

"Aubrey!" She said quietly.

Aubrey turned to see Elizabeth, in the dim light; Aubrey's face ran every emotion imaginable. She was angry yet sad and very frighten.

"Aubrey, baby, its mommy. Sweetheart, come away from the edge, come to mommy Elizabeth said in a low calming voice. Aubrey moved closer to the edge.

"Baby please. Get away from the cliff baby, please. Come on, let's go back home and go to sleep, baby you have got to be hungry. Let's go home and get a bath alright."

"Please mommy, don't come closer."

The calmness of her voice scared Elizabeth. Out the corner of her eye, Elizabeth saw a movement near the shade of the trees.

Holding tightly to Mark's hand she asked "who are you and what do you want?" The figure didn't say anything.

Finding Love

"Answer me, who are you and what do you want?"

Nothing still, but he stepped out of the shadow of trees. She couldn't make out his face very well until he stepped into moon light.

"Oh my" Elizabeth couldn't finish!

The face of the stranger was that of Aubrey, how can he be related to her, they were told that Aubrey's father was dead and the adoption papers were final. Aubrey is her daughter.

"WHO ARE YOU? She said with authority.

His expression went blank. And he opened his mouth to say something. But nothing came out. It was like he didn't have a voice.

"I demand an answer!" Elizabeth began to scream.

She could hear Mark talking to the staff. She couldn't make out everything that was said, but she heard something about attacking. That she understood very clearly. The question was; did the man hear it also? He stood there with a smile on his face. What was the smirking about she thought. He walked toward Elizabeth, but before he could

Jessica Lara

get any closer it was wasn't just a conversation between Elizabeth and the man. It was a conversation between the man and Mark.

"The Queen asked you a question, who are you and what do you want" he said angrily. The man spoke for the first time but not to her, he addressed the King in a low controlled voice. Again the tension was too great and Elizabeth only saw darkness.

The next thing Elizabeth knew was she laying in their bed with little Aubrey on one side and Mark on the other, his arms across her stomach sleeping. A comfortable smile lit the corners of her mouth and she fell back asleep. She had a lot of questions on her mind rising from the bed and discovering her husband and daughter were missing. Going downstairs, she found her family having breakfast. Mark catching her eyes touched his daughter's arm and pointed over her shoulder. Smiling her biggest smile, "mommy" she yelled, running and wrapping her arms around Elizabeth. Queen Myra was watching everything from the sidelines. She was overjoyed that her family was complete again.

Finding Love

"I love you Aubrey" Elizabeth whispered into her ear.

"I love you too mommy" she said turning and facing the King.

"I love you too daddy and I love you grammie"

"I love you, too Aubrey" the King said. Queen Myra set with tears in her eyes, smiling and said "I love each of you very much".

Aubrey holding Elizabeth's face between her hands, "come on mommy, let's have breakfast". Sitting down to breakfast was more than breakfast, it was a family affair. The staff stayed close. Elizabeth was very happy. Suddenly she was very dizzy and her stomach was in an uproar. She had to leave the table in a flash. The king was right behind her. "Lizy, sweetheart are you okay. You look faint". Almost in the same breath he orders Petra to call Doctor Cyrus.

Mark put Elizabeth back to bed and waited patiently for the doctor to come. The staff bustled around trying to stay out the way but their concern about the queen was very apparent. Doctor Cyrus talked with Elizabeth and took her temperature.

He also checked her vital signs. Elizabeth was given orders to stay in bed and rest for the remainder of the day. Aubrey and Queen Myra paid her a visit throughout the day. The King finished working in his office would often take the time out to come by and check on her. Elizabeth was very bored and wanted to get out of bed, but everyone made her follow the doctor's orders. Queen Myra had a secret but she wanted the doctor to confirm what she suspected. The next morning. Elizabeth found a familiar face glancing at her with a smile. "Morning sweetheart" he smiles. "Morning Honey!" She responded. He smiled and kissed her on the lips and then on the forehead and said "I'll be right back!" Few seconds later he was back as promised with a tray with two covers. We were eating breakfast in bed how thoughtful, she thought.

They spent the rest of the morning in that same bed just talking and eating. Eventually Aubrey came in very excited and very happy. "Mommy! Mommy! Daddy! Daddy!" Aubrey yelled as she jumped up and down on the bed.

Finding Love

"Yes!" Elizabeth said.

"Yes, Aubrey!" Mark said.

"Guess what day it is..." She smiled her big smile at Mark and Elizabeth.

It took a second for her to remember but Elizabeth managed to say "happy birthday Aubrey!"

"You remembered mommy!"

"Of course baby!"

"Happy birthday, Aubrey!" Mark said as he tickled her in Elizabeth's arms.

"Thank you, daddy!"

"You're welcome baby; the staff has worked very hard to prepare a great party for you. Have you thought about what you want for your birthday? With everything that has happened we didn't have the time to do a lot of shopping but we can go together later. "Mommy, grammie said she has a secret, but she told me and that's what I want for my birthday. "

Elizabeth looked at little Aubrey's face, she was so very confused about what Aubrey was talking about. "Well baby, mommy will do everything in her powers to give you what you want. Tell mommy what you want sweetheart?"

"I want a baby sister, grammie said you're going to have a baby oh but that's a secret. Don't tell grammie I told you okay."

Doctor Cyrus confirmed what Queen Myra suspected. Both King Mark and Queen Elizabeth were more than excited about the good news. The doctor than allowed Elizabeth to get out of bed and they were able to take Audrey to the market to shop for her early birthday present.

***

When they arrived at the market Aubrey ran from store to store trying to find the perfect early birthday present. "Mommy, mommy, daddy, daddy, I want this one, please may I keep him?"

There in the window of the pet store was a little black puppy with a white star over his right eye. The puppy was very lively, jumping around and wagging his tail. "Mommy can I have him, please mommy!"

Finding Love

Elizabeth looked at the puppy for awhile and thought he can be a good watch dog when he gets older. She never wanted to experience loosing Aubrey again so the dog would be a good buy. Looking at the King, Elizabeth told Mark of her thoughts and he readily agreed. Aubrey, Elizabeth, and Mark toss around names for the puppy. It was agreed because of his color, his name should be chocolate.

Their family began to grow. Eight months later Elizabeth gave birth to twins. A boy for Mark and a little sister for Aubrey. The announcement of the new royal prince and princess went throughout the whole nation. Queen Elizabeth finally felt Infinite love, from her husband, Aubrey, Myra and she was accepted by the staff and all the ruling classes. Mark came in to watch her sleep only to see that the queen was wide awake. Lying in the bed next to her, Mark said "Queen Elizabeth, I always knew you were beautiful, I am so happy you took the dare and remained in the palace the first two years. I thank God that our years together will

Jessica Lara

always be filled with love. I dedicate my life to you." Elizabeth then presses her lips against his.

"I love you sweetheart, I love you!"

Made in the USA
Lexington, KY
29 October 2012